taking responsibility for
your life

because nobody else will

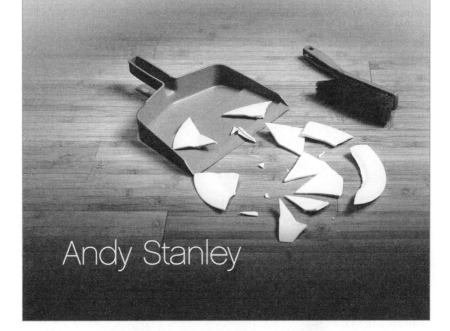

Andy Stanley

ZONDERVAN®

NORTH POINT
RESOURCES

ZONDERVAN.com/
AUTHORTRACKER
follow your favorite authors

ZONDERVAN

Taking Responsibility for Your Life Participant's Guide
Copyright © 2011 by North Point Ministries, Inc.

Requests for information should be addressed to:

Zondervan, *Grand Rapids, Michigan 49530*

ISBN 978-0-310-89440-7

Cover and interior design: Brian Manley (funwithrobots.com)

Printed in the United States of America

13 14 15 16 /DCI/ 20 19 18 17 16 15 14 13 12 11 10 9 8 7

CONTENTS

INTRODUCTION

Who Takes It Seriously?

by Andy Stanley

When my kids were much younger, and I'd see wet towels they had left lying on the floor, sometimes I would stand by the towels and call for the kids. When they came, I'd calmly say, "I'd like you to say this to me: 'Dad, please pick up my towel and hang it up for me in the bathroom, because I was too lazy to do it myself."

Now I'm not suggesting you do that with your kids; this video series isn't about parenting. Who knows, the experts might even say that what I did was pretty weak as far as healthy parenting goes. I guess time will tell.

But I just wanted to help my kids get a clearer picture of responsibility. I wanted to help them grasp the concept that being irresponsible isn't just a personal matter; it impacts anybody and everybody who's connected to us.

Nothing Neutral About It

Irresponsibility is not a neutral thing; it isn't something that just sits on the floor and can be ignored.

When we shirk our responsibilities, in essence we're expecting other people to carry the burden of the messes or the chaos that we've created. That's just the built-in nature and dynamics of irresponsibility.

What's worse, irresponsibility is contagious, especially when we see other people who seem to be getting away with it.

The Fulfillment You Were Made For

But you know, responsibility has its own built-in nature and dynamics as well, and they're awesome. The fact is, we were *made* for responsibility. And we're actually the most fulfilled when our lives are filled with it and we're being faithful to those obligations.

Think about it. When you have something important to do, and you're doing a good job at it, don't you just feel better about yourself? For example, one of the most encouraging things a mother can hear is her husband saying, "You know, honey, you're an incredible mother to our kids!"

It's also why it's such a struggle for a family guy to be out of work. It's agonizing, it's depressing, and it drives him crazy—because he wants to faithfully fulfill the responsibility that he knows is his.

We all feel better when we're doing that—and we were *designed* to feel that way. It's just the way God wired us. Again, he created us to be responsible, and we're all happiest and most fulfilled when we're doing a good job at that.

I can say I've never met an irresponsible person who's happy. I've met plenty who can make an incredible case for "it's not my fault." But even after they make their cases, there are no smiles on their faces.

Lots of Questions

So it makes you wonder: Where does our tendency toward irresponsibility come from? Irresponsibility seems to be running rampant in our culture—why is that?

What's our responsibility toward the irresponsible? It just doesn't seem fair that their negligence or carelessness should bring a burden on those around them. Is there anything we can do about that?

And what help should we expect from God on this issue? Can we honestly expect him to "cover" for us when we've been irresponsible? Is it wrong to pray for his help in cleaning up the messes we've made?

Moving Forward

Responsibilities . . . we all have them. But we don't always take them as seriously as we should.

Wouldn't it be great if we really took responsibility for the things we're responsible for? It's time to stop pointing fingers and making excuses. It's time to take out the "ir" in *irresponsibility*. Let's find out how.

SESSION 1

Let the Blames Begin

Irresponsibility isn't a difficult concept to grasp. It's simply when I don't take responsibility for whatever I'm responsible for.

While irresponsibility is easy to spot in others, it's almost impossible to see in the mirror. In some ways our entire culture is becoming less and less responsible; increasingly in our day, irresponsibility is almost celebrated. People have even discovered ways to profit from their irresponsibility. In such an environment, irresponsibility *thrives*.

Some people will even claim, in effect, "I have the right to be irresponsible—I can do and say whatever I want. No one has the right to hold me accountable. And others are responsible to clean up whatever messes I create through my irresponsibility."

Deep down, we all know how damaging irresponsibility is. If that's something we can change ... shouldn't we?

DISCUSSION STARTER

What to you are the most glaring examples of irresponsibility in our culture today?

Why is this rampant irresponsibility so troubling? Why does it matter?

VIDEO OVERVIEW

For Session 1 of the DVD

Am I taking responsibility for my life ... *really?*"

Irresponsibility—whether it's in our family, our workplace, our church, our community, or our nation—is contagious. That's especially so when we see people getting away with being irresponsible, and even being rewarded for it.

Whenever anyone acts irresponsibly, somebody has to come along and shoulder the burden of his or her irresponsibility.

Irresponsibility isn't a solo thing; it always impacts whoever's connected to the person who's irresponsible. Irresponsibility is ultimately a community matter, a family matter, a corporate matter.

All of us at times want to shirk our responsibilities. But followers of Jesus know that they must not do this, because they're ultimately accountable to their heavenly Father. Christians should be the most responsible people on the planet, since they understand the connectedness of their families and communities and culture.

In the Bible, the early chapters of Genesis show us when irresponsibility was introduced into the human race. We read in Genesis 1 that God gave responsibility for the earth's care to the man and woman he had created. Along with that responsibility, he gave them a single prohibition to stay away from a certain tree. This was before humankind sinned and many centuries before God gave his people the Ten Commandments. In the beginning, there was just one rule and a lot of responsibility.

Again, God designed us to be responsible. We know this intuitively. We're happiest when we're being responsible.

In Genesis, we see that as soon as Adam and Eve sinned, they threw off their accountability to God. They felt ashamed and tried to hide from him.

God confronted Adam first about this; he was holding Adam accountable. Adam could have responded, "Yes, I take full responsibility for everything. Do with me as you will." But instead he blamed Eve—who said it wasn't her fault either. The blame game began.

Irresponsibility always creates conflict—not only interpersonal conflict, but conflict within us as we try to hide our guilt.

Our culture is full of people who live every single day with the weight of shame and guilt over the irresponsible behavior that they've blamed their way out of and for which no one has held them accountable.

VIDEO NOTES

_____

_____

_____

_____

_____

_____

_____

_____

_____

_____

_____

_____

_____

_____

_____

_____

_____

_____

_____

DISCUSSION QUESTIONS

1. "Am I taking responsibility for my life ... *really?*" At this point in your life, how would you answer that question?

2. Do you ever feel you have a right to be irresponsible, that you can do and say whatever you want and no one can hold you accountable? When are you most tempted to feel this way, and why?

3. As you look at others around you, in what ways do you see irresponsibility being rewarded? How does this affect you?

4. In what significant ways have you experienced the truth that we're happiest when we're doing a good job at something we're responsible for?

5. What do you consider to be your most significant areas of responsibility in life?

6. How have you seen personally that irresponsibility creates conflict—both within ourselves and with others around us? If so, what have you learned from this?

MILEPOSTS

- Having responsibilities is God's design for us, and we're most fulfilled when we're managing that responsibility well.

- In a group or community of any size, when people are taking responsibility seriously, lots of rules aren't needed.

- Whenever someone is irresponsible, that irresponsibility eventually becomes someone else's responsibility. Our irresponsibility always impacts others.

MOVING FORWARD

Think about Andy's suggested assignments in this week's teaching.

First, listen to your words. In any area of life, do you try to shift responsibility off yourself?

Second, as you experience relational conflict at work, at home, or with neighbors or friends—whenever you run into relational conflict of any sort—think of a circle that represents all the blame for that conflict. Then ask yourself, "What part of it am I ultimately responsible for?"

CHANGING YOUR MIND

As a reminder of the way God designed us for taking responsibility,

reflect on the amazing truth of these words spoken by God to our

first human parents:

> *God blessed them and said to them,*
> *"Be fruitful and increase in number;*
> *fill the earth and subdue it.*
> *Rule over the fish in the sea and the birds in the sky*
> *and over every living creature that moves on the ground."*
> *Genesis 1:28*

PREPARATION FOR SESSION 2

To help you prepare for Session 2, use these suggested devotions during the week leading up to your small group meeting.

Day One

In the New Testament, read Galatians 6:1–10. Focus especially on verses 1 and 2. What do we learn here about our obligations toward others?

Day Two

Read Galatians 6:1–10. Today, think especially about verses 3 and 4. What do we learn here about comparing ourselves with others and about self-deception?

Day Three

Look over Galatians 6:1–10 again. Reflect especially on verse 5. What do we learn here about our obligations toward ourselves?

Day Four

Read Galatians 6:1–10, and today focus especially on verses 7 and 8. How does God emphasize the truth that people reap what they sow? How do you emphasize the importance of that principle coming through in this passage?

Day Five

Read Galatians 6:1–10. Look closely at verses 9 and 10. How do these verses communicate the advantage we receive from reaping what we sow? And what does our "sowing" involve, according to this passage?

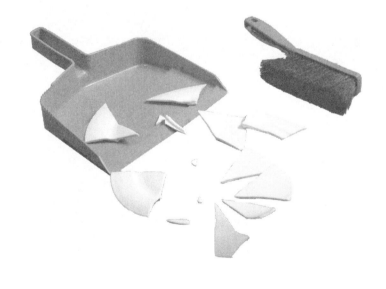

Last Session

By God's design, we're happiest when we're doing a good job at managing the responsibilities we've been given. When we're irresponsible, that's bad news not only for us, but also for others. Our irresponsibility always impacts those who are connected to us.

SESSION 2

The Disproportionate Life

Remember the Archimedes principle? Discovered by the ancient Greek mathematician Archimedes, this principle explains the buoyancy of water—why and how things float. As we see it in action today, it explains why the ocean waves will lift up vessels far heavier and larger than anything Archimedes ever dreamed of, like today's giant cargo ships and aircraft carriers. By leveraging this principle, countless vessels navigate the world's waterways every day. But whenever the principle is compromised in some way, they sink.

The same holds true with the principle underlying the dynamics of responsibility and irresponsibility. And though it usually slides to the periphery of our thinking, it's worth keeping regularly in focus. If we leverage this principle, the outcome is a gift. If we ignore it, the outcome seems like a punishment.

So how do we make the most of responsibility?

DISCUSSION STARTER

To what degree would we say our lives today are influenced by the actions and choices from our pasts?

VIDEO OVERVIEW

For Session 2 of the DVD

It was Archimedes in ancient Greece who first discovered and described the principle of buoyancy and fluid displacement.

As a principle, it's neither good nor bad; it just is. People can leverage it for positive things, or they can ignore it and face the consequences. That's the nature of the principle.

Here's another principle: *People reap what they sow.* That's always been true and always will be.

This biblical principle explains why our irresponsibility eventually becomes somebody else's responsibility. And it's why our irresponsibility always catches up with us.

Like Archimedes' principle, this biblical principle is one you can leverage for good, or you can ignore it and face the consequences.

In the Bible, we find this principle in Galatians 6. As the apostle Paul discusses our responsibility to help others as well as our need to take responsibility for ourselves, he shows us that helping others is never meant to be an excuse for acting irresponsibly in our own lives.

Paul mentions self-deception here. It's especially easy to deceive ourselves when we compare ourselves to others. It's so easy to cut ourselves too much slack and become irresponsible.

Warning us not to be deceived, Paul reminds us: "God cannot be mocked" (Galatians 6:7). He can't be outwitted, outsmarted, or fooled. Whatever irresponsibility we try to hide, God sees. If we're unwilling to carry our own loads, we'll never get by with that in the end. God is always aware of our irresponsibility, whether it's with our money, our family, our morality, our ethics, or whatever.

With that warning, Paul brings in this basic principle: "People reap what they sow" (Galatians 6:7). It's something we all intuitively recognize as being true. We see how life is connected—that where we are today is a result of past decisions, and where we'll be tomorrow is connected to our choices and actions today.

God loves us so much that he lets us know about this principle ahead of time. It's a principle we can allow to work *for* us.

We reap what we sow. We reap *later* and *greater*. The reaping might not come for days, or weeks, or months, or years—but eventually it will come. And the reaping will be "greater." It will seem bigger than you can imagine. The consequences of our irresponsibility will be worse than you think is just or fair.

So we're duly warned.

VIDEO NOTES

_____

_____

_____

_____

_____

_____

_____

_____

_____

_____

_____

_____

_____

_____

_____

_____

_____

_____

_____

DISCUSSION QUESTIONS

1. "People reap what they sow"—what are some important ways that you've already been taught that principle, either by others or simply by the experiences of life?

2. Why is it so easy to deceive ourselves when we compare ourselves with others?

3. When you hear the biblical admonition to "carry [your] own load" (Galatians 6:5), what do you think of? For you, what's the "load" you need to be most concerned about?

4. What does it mean to you that "God cannot be mocked" (Galatians 6:7)? Why is that instruction needed? In what ways do people try to "mock" God?

5. When you think of the fact that God sees—clearly and immediately—every instance of our irresponsibility, how do you react?

6. Looking back on your life, how do you recognize the truth that who you are today is a result of your past decisions and actions?

MILEPOSTS

- The principle of sowing and reaping is what drives the dynamics surrounding responsibility and irresponsibility. We reap what we sow.

- We reap *later*—the reaping might not come for days, weeks, months, even years. But eventually it will come.

- We reap *greater*—the reaping will seem bigger than we could have imagined. For our irresponsibility, the reaping will seem worse than we think is fair.

MOVING FORWARD

We reap what we sow—let the powerful truth of that principle motivate you in your current actions. What's the most important "sowing" you can be doing in your life at this time? Think about the most significant areas of your life. What are the most important habits you want to have in place for each one?

CHANGING YOUR MIND

This session's key Scripture passage is a reminder of the driving principle behind all the dynamics related to responsibility and irresponsibility:

Do not be deceived: God cannot be mocked.
People reap what they sow.
Galatians 6:7

PREPARATION FOR SESSION 3

To help you prepare for Session 3, use these suggested devotions during the week leading up to your small group meeting.

Day One

Glance over the story of the fall of Jericho in Joshua 6. How does God demonstrate to his people that they need to trust in him, not in their military, as they proceed to conquer the Promised Land?

Day Two

Read what happens in Joshua 7:1–5 as the Israelites attempt to conquer a second city, Ai. Notice how the reason for what happened is mentioned first, before the account of the events themselves. Why was this important?

Day Three

Read in Joshua 7:6–9 about the response of Joshua and the leaders in the aftermath of their defeat at Ai. What are the most significant thoughts going through their minds?

Day Four

In Joshua 7:10–15, read God's response to Joshua regarding this situation. What are the most important things God is communicating here?

Day Five

In Joshua 7:16–26, read how Joshua and the people responded to what God had revealed to them. How do these things indicate the seriousness of the situation? What were the most important lessons they were to take away from this incident?

Last Session

We reap what we sow. That's the driving principle behind the dynamics of responsibility and irresponsibility. We reap later, and we reap greater.

SESSION 3

This Is No Time to Pray

In this session we'll look at an Old Testament story that reveals surprising perspectives on responsibility and irresponsibility.

As we do, I wonder if you might be in one of these three groups of people:

1. Some religious people will tend to mask their irresponsibility with prayer and religious talk.

2. When it comes to dealing with the irresponsibility of others, some people have misguided compassion. Instead of holding others accountable, they'll actually facilitate their irresponsibility.

3. Lots of people who've been responsible themselves—who've sown the right seeds—will nevertheless be discouraged or burdened because they feel they're reaping the negative effects of someone else's irresponsibility.

The story from the Bible that we'll look at in this session focuses on one person's single act of irresponsibility—and yet the consequences of his actions were immediate and crushing for an entire nation. What wisdom and help can that story offer the people in those three categories mentioned above?

Let's find out.

DISCUSSION STARTER

When have you ever tried to pray your way out of the consequences of some irresponsibility? What kind of answer did you get from God?

VIDEO OVERVIEW

For Session 3 of the DVD

In the Old Testament, Joshua followed Moses as Israel's leader, taking the Israelites across the Jordan River into the Promised Land. This fulfilled the promise God made 650 years earlier, that this land would be given to Abraham's descendants. Finally, after centuries of slavery in Egypt, Joshua led the people into this land.

By then it was already populated by pagan cultures that were extremely evil—they sacrificed children to pagan gods, and their women were treated with unspeakable horror. God in essence was saying, "I gave them time to right their wrongs, but they did not; it's best now that these cultures be eradicated."

The first pagan city that God's people encountered was Jericho. God made their conquest of Jericho easy, showing them their need to trust in him.

They came next to the much smaller city of Ai. The Israelites expected a quick conquest here. However, one Israelite man had violated God's instructions by secretly taking silver and gold from Jericho.

The soldiers of Ai promptly routed Israel's forces. This shocked and frightened Israel. In grief, Joshua and other leaders fell on their faces in prayer. But God commanded Joshua to get up, and asked why he was facedown on the ground. God informed Joshua of the sin that had occurred and gave instructions for discovering who had done it. He emphasized that Israel could not stand before her enemies until the stolen treasures were destroyed. In essence God was saying, "This isn't the time to pray."

The story dramatically shows what happens when one member of a community acts irresponsibly. Everybody connected to the guilty person eventually reaps what he has sown.

From our perspective, that doesn't seem fair, but that's the nature of irresponsibility. We're connected, and one person's irresponsibility eventually becomes everyone's responsibility.

That's why we must learn to confront those among us who are

acting irresponsibly. The most loving thing we can do for them is to refuse to put up with their irresponsibility.

Arising from this story in Joshua 7 is this question for all religious people: "Are you hiding behind your prayers? Are you praying when you need to stand up and do something?"

If God has already addressed an issue in his Word, then we don't need to pray about it. We've already been told what to do.

Likewise, if we're trying to pray our way out of something we behaved our way into, it's time not to pray but to stand up and do something. Prayer is no substitute for taking responsibility.

VIDEO NOTES

_____

_____

_____

_____

_____

_____

_____

_____

_____

_____

_____

_____

_____

_____

_____

_____

_____

_____

DISCUSSION QUESTIONS

1. Can you think of any instances in your life when you've tried to mask your irresponsibility with prayer and religious talk? If so, what was going on in your mind and heart?

2. Andy speaks of "misguided compassion," when we facilitate the irresponsibility of others instead of holding them accountable. Do you find this to be a tendency in your life? If so, why do you tend to respond this way to the irresponsibility of others?

3. In what ways, if any, have you felt that you're bearing the burden caused by the irresponsibility of others?

4. Do you ever find yourself tempted to blame God in a situation involving human irresponsibility (either your own or that of others)? If so, what causes you to feel this way?

5. Why do you think it's so difficult for many of us in our culture to confront the irresponsibility of others?

6. Think about the groups of people you're involved with. What do you consider to be your most important responsibilities toward them? How can you strategically set an example for them of acting responsibly?

MILEPOSTS

- In the things we're dealing with in various areas of our lives, there comes a point when it's time to stand up and take responsibility.

- We can easily hide behind prayer and religious talk when what we really need to do is stand up and do something. Prayer is no substitute for being responsible.

- We must learn not to tolerate irresponsibility in others who are close to us. The most loving thing to do for them is to refuse to put up with their irresponsibility.

MOVING FORWARD

In what specific areas of your life do you need to stand up now and take responsibility?

Think about the people in your circle of relationships. Are any of them negatively impacting you and others because of their irresponsibility? If so, how should you be confronting this situation?

CHANGING YOUR MIND

Use this week's key Scripture passage as a reminder that prayer is no substitute for taking responsibility:

> The LORD said to Joshua, "Stand up!
> What are you doing down on your face?"
> Joshua 7:10

PREPARATION FOR SESSION 4

To help you prepare for Session 4, use these suggested devotions during the week leading up to your small group meeting.

Day One

In your Bible, glance over the parable Jesus told in Matthew 25:14–30. In the story's setup in verses 14 and 15, what are the most important details?

Day Two

Read the story Jesus tells in Matthew 25:14–30. In verses 16–18, what are the most important details concerning the actions taken by these three servants?

Day Three

Look over Matthew 25:14–30. This time, reflect especially on what happens in verses 19–23. What truths do these things reflect about responsibility and faithfulness?

Day Four

Read Jesus' story in Matthew 25:14–30. Today, focus especially on verses 24–27. What is most significant in the servant's words? And what is most significant in his master's reply?

Day Five

Read Matthew 25:14–30. Look closely at the conclusion of the story in verses 28–30. What important takeaway does Jesus offer us from his story?

Last Session

In whatever we're dealing with in various areas of our lives, there comes a point when it's time to stand up and take responsibility. Prayer and religious talk are no substitutes for being responsible.

SESSION 4

Embracing Your Response Ability

Some of our favorite stories are about people who seem to have very limited opportunities. Early on, they could have easily (and correctly) complained, "Life's not fair!" They might even have used that as an excuse to forget about pursuing responsible and productive lives. But instead they chose not to make excuses, and to leverage what they *did* have for the benefit of others.

"It's not fair!" In every home, every child at some point has made that complaint. And in every generation, in all countries and cultures, parents and grandparents look right back at them and respond, "*Life's* not fair."

They're right about that. Yet there's something in all of us that *wants* life to be fair. Although, to be honest, we're generally most concerned about unfairness when we're on the short end of the stick. Funny how we don't think about it when we receive more benefits and blessings than others do—others who probably deserve just as much or more than we deserve.

So how should we understand and deal with life's unfairness? Where can we get further perspective from God on this?

DISCUSSION STARTER

How strong is your inner sense of wanting life to be fair? Is it something you often feel?

When have you been most aware of life's *un*fairness? When have you been most troubled by it?

VIDEO OVERVIEW

For Session 4 of the DVD

Life isn't fair—there's an unevenness about it. And this can quickly become an excuse for our irresponsibility.

The issue isn't how we can make life more fair or even. The real question is this: What will I do with the opportunities I've been given by life and by God?

In Matthew 25:14–30, Jesus relates a parable to show us that God doesn't try to fix the unevenness and the unfairness of life. Instead, he wants us to learn to leverage it.

His story concerns a man going on a long journey who first entrusts his wealth to three servants, expecting them to invest it.

They receive differing amounts. But even the one getting the least had a fortune—one "talent" (the Greek word Jesus used is *tálanton*), or a "bag of gold" (TNIV). The amount was equivalent to twenty years' wages for a typical laborer. Another servant received five talents and another two.

Afterward, the servants receiving five and two talents both doubled the investments. But the servant with one talent dug a hole and buried it.

Finally the master returned to settle accounts with them. The two servants reporting a doubled investment were each told, "Well done, good and faithful servant! You have been faithful with a few things; I will put you in charge of many things. Come and share your master's happiness!" (Matthew 25:21, 23).

Then the third servant reported that he'd buried his money because of his fear of his master's toughness. Essentially, he was blaming the master.

The master rebuked him for his laziness and worthlessness. And the money the servant buried was taken away and given to the servant who already had ten talents.

We learn in this parable that those who've been responsible with what they have will be given more.

As Jesus wraps up the story, the master commands that the "worthless servant" be thrown "outside, into the darkness, where there will be weeping and gnashing of teeth" (25:30). This "gnashing of teeth" was the sign of acute frustration. That's the tragic consequence for those who are irresponsible, who waste the opportunities given them.

The point of this parable is this: We don't all get the same amount of opportunity, but we're all held accountable for what we do with whatever we're given. These opportunities are on loan to us, and it's our responsibility to figure out how to leverage them to their maximum.

The bottom line: To whom something is given—regardless of how great or small—something is required.

VIDEO NOTES

_____

_____

_____

_____

_____

_____

_____

_____

_____

_____

_____

_____

_____

_____

_____

_____

_____

_____

_____

DISCUSSION QUESTIONS

1. In your own life, or in observing others, how have you seen most vividly the truth that irresponsibility diminishes our happiness?

2. "The more we have, the more we waste"—how have you seen this to be true, either in your life or in others around you?

3. What do you consider to be the most strategic opportunities God has given you?

4. Think of the people around you, the people you know best. How can you show appreciation, support, and encouragement for them as they seek to make the most of the opportunities they've been given?

5. Why do you think it's important to understand that the opportunities and responsibilities we've been given are *on loan* to us from God? How should that impact our mindsets toward our obligations?

6. What does it mean personally to you that we're held accountable by God for the opportunities and responsibilities that we've been given?

MILEPOSTS

- We're all given differing amounts of opportunities and re-sponsibilities. The unevenness of this might seem unfair. But that's just the way life is.

- Sometimes we use this unevenness, this seeming unfair-ness, as an excuse for acting irresponsibly. But that is wrong.

- We're responsible for making the most of whatever opportu-nities we've been given, large or small.

MOVING FORWARD

What are the significant opportunities you have been given? How are you leveraging them for all they're worth? What can you do to lever-age them even more?

Are you focusing on being responsible with those opportunities and avoiding the tendency to compare yourself with other people and what they've been given?

What can help you avoid the tendency to gripe and complain and to make excuses for being irresponsible?

CHANGING YOUR MIND

Listen carefully to these words of Jesus (which he placed in the mouth of the master in this parable). Let these words remind you of the consequences both of responsibility and of irresponsibility.

For those who have will be given more,
and they will have an abundance.
As for those who do not have,
even what they have will be taken from them.
Matthew 25:29

Leader's Guide

So, You're the Leader...

Is that intimidating? Perhaps exciting? No doubt you have some mental pictures of what it will look like, what you will say, and how it will go. Before you get too far into the planning process, there are some things you should know about leading a small group discussion. We've compiled some tried and true techniques here to help you.

Basics About Leading

1. Cultivate discussion — It's easy to think that the meeting lives or dies by your ideas. In reality, the ideas of everyone in the group are what make a small group meeting successful. The most valuable thing you can do is to get people to share their thoughts. That's how the relationships in your group will grow and thrive. Here's a rule: The impact of your study material will typically never exceed the impact of the relationships through which it was studied. The more meaningful the relationships, the more meaningful the study. In a sterile environment, even the best material is suppressed.

2. Point to the material — A good host or hostess gets the party going by offering delectable hors d'oeuvres and beverages. You too should be ready to serve up "delicacies" from the material. Sometimes you will simply read the discussion questions and invite everyone to respond. At other times, you will encourage others to share their ideas. Remember, some of the best treats are the ones your guests will bring to the party. Go with the flow of the meeting, and be ready to pop out of the kitchen as needed.

3. Depart from the material — A talented ministry team has carefully designed this study for your small group. But that doesn't mean you should follow every part word for word. Knowing how and when to depart from the material is a valuable art. Nobody knows more about your people than you do. The narratives, questions, and exercises are here to provide a framework for discovery. However, every group is motivated differently. Sometimes the best way to start a small group discussion is simply to ask, "Does anyone have a personal insight or revelation they'd like to share from this week's material?" Then sit back and listen.

4. Stay on track — Conversation is the currency of a small group discussion. The more interchange, the healthier the "economy." However, you need to keep your objectives in mind. If your goal is to have a meaningful experience with this material, then you should make sure the discussion is contributing to that end. It's easy to get off on a tangent. Be prepared to interject politely and refocus the group. You might need to say something like, "Excuse me, we're obviously all interested in this subject; however, I just want to make sure we cover all the material for this week."

5. Above all, pray — The best communicators are the ones that manage to get out of God's way enough to let him communicate *through* them. That's important to keep in mind. Books don't teach God's Word; neither do sermons nor group discussions. God himself speaks into the hearts of men and women, and prayer is our vital channel to communicate directly with him. Cover your efforts in prayer. You don't just want God present at your meeting; you want him to direct it.

We hope you find these suggestions helpful. And we hope you enjoy leading this study. You will find additional guidelines and suggestions for each session in the Leader's Guide notes that follow.

Leader's Guide
Session Notes

Session 1 — LET THE BLAMES BEGIN
Bottom Line

We can credit God's design of humanity for the fact that we're most fulfilled when we're doing a good job at managing the responsibilities we've been given. But whenever we act irresponsibly, it always negatively impacts those who are connected to us. Our irresponsibility is never a solo affair.

Discussion Starter

Use the "Discussion Starter" printed in Session 1 of the Participant's Guide to "break the ice"—and to help everyone see the destructiveness and total undesirability of irresponsibility.

Notes for Discussion Questions

1. **"Am I taking responsibility for my life ... *really*?" At this point in your life, how would you answer that question?**
   This question comes up in each video session of Andy's teaching. It's meant to be one that we continually reflect on, continually refining our answers.

2. **Do you ever feel you have a right to be irresponsible, that you can do and say whatever you want and no one can hold you accountable? When are you most tempted to feel this way, and why?**

Most of us have times when we feel this way. Encourage honest discussion about it.

3. **As you look at others around you, in what ways do you see irresponsibility being rewarded? How does this affect you?**

Help guide the discussion toward the truth that what gets rewarded gets repeated.

4. **In what significant ways have you experienced the truth that we're happiest when we're doing a good job at something we're responsible for?**

Allow plenty of time here to reflect fully on the joys of responsible living.

5. **What do you consider to be your most significant areas of responsibility in life?**

Again, allow plenty of time for this, since for all of us, our areas of responsibility are multifaceted and far-reaching.

6.   **How have you seen personally that irresponsibility creates conflict—both within ourselves and with others around us? If so, what have you learned from this?**

This is something we've all experienced. Focus the discussion on the takeaway—the lessons we can learn from these situations, rather than the details involved.

Moving Forward

The goal here is to encourage the group members to give plenty of thought in the days and weeks ahead to the obvious signs in their lives indicating their sense of responsibility, as well as their tendencies toward irresponsibility.

Preparation for Session 2

Remember to point out the brief daily devotions that the group members can complete and which will help greatly in stimulating discussion in your next session. These devotions will enable everyone to dig into the Bible and start wrestling with the topics that will come up next time.

Session 2 — THE DISPROPORTIONATE LIFE

Bottom Line

There is powerful and inescapable truth in the principle that *people reap what they sow.* We can leverage that principle for our good, or ignore it and suffer tragic consequences. So we need all the encouragement we can get to see life's *connectedness*—our todays have been shaped by our yesterdays, and our tomorrows will be determined by our todays.

Discussion Starter

Use the "Discussion Starter" listed for Session 2 of the Participant's Guide. This one should help everyone in your group focus on the powerful and inescapable truth that we reap what we sow.

Notes for Discussion Questions

1. **"People reap what they sow"—what are some important ways that you've already been taught that principle, either by others or simply by the experiences of life?**

    Encourage everyone to think of ways that they've "reaped" both positively and negatively.

2. **Why is it so easy to deceive ourselves when we compare ourselves with others?**

   Help guide the discussion toward the truth of our natural self-centeredness and our extreme vulnerability to self-deception (which is hard for most of us to admit!).

3. **When you hear the biblical admonition to "carry [your] own load" (Galatians 6:5), what do you think of? For you, what's the "load" you need to be most concerned about?**

   The discussion can include many specifics, but also encourage the recognition of the overarching circumstances that shape and determine our responsibilities—our calling to our spouses and families, for example, and to our brothers and sisters in the faith, our work—and above all, our calling to serve and be devoted to God.

4. **What does it mean to you that "God cannot be mocked" (Galatians 6:7)? Why is that instruction needed? In what ways do people ever try to "mock" God?**

   Help guide the discussion toward a higher awareness of God's all-knowingness and full attentiveness, as well as his loving care and concern in all areas of our lives.

5.   **When you think of the fact that God sees—clearly and immediately—every instance of our irresponsibility, how do you react?** Some might be fearful as they think more about this. Help guide the discussion toward a greater awareness of our heavenly Father's total concern and love for every aspect of our lives.

6.   **Looking back on your life, how do you recognize the truth that who you are today is a result of your past decisions and actions?** This might involve some painful recollections. Model and encourage full acceptance of one another, since we all can look back and see decisions and actions we regret.

Moving Forward

The goal here is to deepen everyone's practical awareness—in every area of life—of the principle that we reap what we sow. Understanding this principle well is meant to liberate us toward effective, fruitful action in our lives, with continuing, long-term benefits.

Preparation for Session 3

Again, encourage your group members to complete the brief daily devotions. These will help stimulate discussion in your next session. They'll enable everyone to dig into the Bible and start wrestling with the topics coming up next time.

Session 3 — THIS IS NO TIME TO PRAY

Bottom Line

We should never let religious games become an excuse for avoiding responsibility. There are many occasions in life when we need to hear the admonition to stand up and take responsibility. We also must learn not to tolerate irresponsibility in others, for their sake as well as for the good of everyone around them.

Discussion Starter

Again, make full use of the "Discussion Starter," as listed for Session 3 of the Participant's Guide. This should help the group focus on the kind of religious games we can play when we've been shirking our responsibilities.

Notes for Discussion Questions

1. **Can you think of any instances in your own life when you've tried to mask your irresponsibility with prayer and religious talk? If so, what was going on in your mind and heart?**
    Anyone in the group who has a church background should be able to come up with something here.

2. **Andy speaks of "misguided compassion," when we facilitate the irresponsibility of others instead of holding them accountable. Do you find this to be a tendency in your own life? If so, why do you think you tend to respond this way to the irresponsibility of others?**

    This tendency will probably be more apparent in people who are more naturally caring and compassionate. But we all tend to have certain relationships where this can easily happen.

3. **In what ways, if any, have you felt that you're bearing the burden caused by the irresponsibility of others?**

    Most of us tend to feel such burdens, in one way or another. Keep the focus on how we can respond positively to this kind of situation.

4. **Do you ever find yourself tempted to blame God in a situation involving human irresponsibility (either your own or that of others)? If so, what causes you to feel this way?**

    Help identify the reasons that we mistakenly blame God. Encourage freedom of expression here—though it's true that we're wrong to ever "blame" God, we all do at some point, and God's loving forgiveness is fully available for this as we recognize and confess it.

5. **Why do you think it's so difficult for many of us in our culture to confront the irresponsibility of others?**

   This is more difficult for some people than for others. For those who find it hardest, be careful to avoid making them feel discouraged about this.

6. **Think about the groups of people you're involved with. What do you consider to be your most important responsibilities toward them? How can you strategically set an example for them of acting responsibly?**

   Allow plenty of time to reflect and respond to this. Encourage an active recognition of our interconnectedness with those we live and work with.

Moving Forward

Encourage the group members to recognize one significant area in their lives where they need to take responsible action—or one significant relationship in which they need to confront someone else's irresponsibility.

Preparation for Session 4

Again, encourage your group members to complete the daily devotions. This will help them be better prepared for the topics coming up next time.

Session 4 — EMBRACING YOUR RESPONSE ABILITY

Bottom Line

It's an inescapable fact that not everyone receives the same degree of opportunities and advantages. But that must never be an excuse for our irresponsibility. Whatever opportunities and responsibilities we've been granted are ours to make the most of. That's the secret of finding fulfillment in life and of receiving the rewards that inevitably flow to the faithful.

Discussion Starter

Again, use the "Discussion Starter" listed for Session 4 of the Participant's Guide. This should help everyone focus on the "unevenness" in life that's simply a fact to be faced and not something we can change.

Notes for Discussion Questions

1. **In your own life, or in observing others, how have you seen most vividly the truth that irresponsibility diminishes our happiness?**

    Help everyone realize the crucial importance of this truth. This is a fact that our culture so often tries to hide.

2.   **"The more we have, the more we waste"—how have you seen**

      this to be true, either in your life or in others around you?

      Even those in your group who are relatively poor will have plen-

      ty of areas in their lives where God's blessings and opportuni-

      ties have been abundant. Encourage them to sharpen their ap-

      preciation for these good things, as well as their commitment

      to make the most of them, in faithfulness to God.

3.   **What do you consider to be the most strategic opportunities**

      God has given you?

      Take enough time to help everyone identify these as fully as

      possible.

4.   **Think of the people around you, the people you know best.**

      How can you show appreciation, support, and encourage-

      ment for them as they seek to make the most of the oppor-

      tunities they've been given?

      Encourage this kind of positive awareness of how others

      around us are gifted and blessed.

5.   **Why do you think it's important to understand that the oppor-**

      tunities and responsibilities we've been given are *on loan* to

us from God? How should that impact our mindsets toward our obligations?

Look especially for ways to overcome the temptation to be narrowly self-centered about these things.

6.   **What does it mean personally to you that we're held accountable by God for the opportunities and responsibilities that we've been given?**

Allow each person in the group to articulate this as fully as possible.

Moving Forward

Take time to pray together in grateful acknowledgment of the significant opportunities that each member of your group has been granted by God. Encourage an active embracing of these responsibilities and a refusal to be sidetracked by any "unfair" limitations we might sense in our situations.

Guardrails DVD

Avoiding Regrets in Your Life

Andy Stanley

[Guardrails: a system designed to keep vehicles from straying into dangerous or off-limit areas.]

They're everywhere, but they don't really get much attention . . . until somebody hits one. And then, more often than not, it is a lifesaver.

Ever wonder what it would be like to have guardrails in other areas of your life—areas where culture baits you to the edge of disaster and then chastises you when you step across the line?

Your friendships. Your finances. Your marriage. Maybe your greatest regret could have been avoided if you had established guardrails.

In this six-session video based study, Andy Stanley challenges us to stop flirting with disaster and establish some personal guardrails.

Session titles:
1. Direct and Protect
2. Why Can't We Be Friends?
3. Flee Baby Flee!
4. Me and the Mrs.
5. The Consumption Assumption
6. Once and For All

Your Move

Four Questions to Ask When You Don't Know What to Do

Andy Stanley

We are all faced with decisions that we never anticipated having to make. And, we usually have to make them quickly. In this four session video group study, author and pastor Andy Stanley discusses four questions that will help participants make sound decisions with God's help. Follow Andy as he teaches how every decision and its outcomes become a permanent part of your story, what to do when you feel the need to pause before taking action, and how to make more of this life by making sound decisions.

The DVD-ROM and separate participant's guide contain everything you need to create your group experience:

Staying in Love

Falling in Love Is Easy, Staying in Love Requires a Plan

Andy Stanley

We all know what's required to fall in love...a pulse. Falling in love is easy. But staying there—that's something else entirely. With more than a thousand matchmaking services available today and new ones springing up all the time, finding a romantic match can be easier than ever. But staying together with the one you've found seems to be the real challenge.

So, is it possible for two people to fall in love and actually stay there? Absolutely! Let pastor and author Andy Stanley show you how in this four-session, video-based study that also features a separate participant's guide.

Session titles include:
1. The Juno Dilemma
2. Re-Modeling
3. Feelin' It
4. Multiple Choice Marriage

Faith, Hope, and Luck

Discover What You Can Expect from God

Andy Stanley

Our faith in God often hinges on his activity—or inactivity—in our daily experiences. When our prayers are answered, our faith soars. When God is silent, it becomes harder to trust him. When God shows up in an unmistakable way, our confidence in him reaches new heights. But when he doesn't come through, our confidence often wanes.

But it doesn't have to be that way—it's not supposed to be that way.

This five-session study is guaranteed to transform your thinking about faith. As you listen or watch, you will discover the difference between faith and hope. You will be presented with a definition of faith that will shed new light on both the Old and New Testaments. Andy Stanley explains what we can expect of God every time we come to him with a request. In addition, he exposes the flaws in what some have labeled The Faith Movement.

With both a DVD and separate participant's guide, *Faith, Hope, and Luck* is not just another group study. This content is foundational for everyone who desires to be an informed, active follower of Christ.

Five sessions include:

1. Better Odds
2. Betting on Hope
3. Beating the Odds
4. No Dice
5. All In

Five Things God Uses to Grow Your Faith

Andy Stanley

Imagine how different your outlook on life would be if you had absolute confidence that God was with you. Imagine how differently you would respond to difficulties, temptations, and even good things if you knew with certainty that God was in all of it and was planning to leverage it for good. In other words, imagine what it would be like to have PERFECT faith. In this DVD study, Andy Stanley builds a biblical case for five things God uses to grow BIG faith.

In six video sessions, Andy covers the following topics:
- Big Faith
- Practical Teaching
- Providential Relationships
- Private Disciplines
- Personal Ministry
- Pivotal Circumstances

Along with the separate participant's guide, this resource will equip groups to become more mature followers of Jesus Christ.

Available in stores and online!

Twisting the Truth

Learning to Discern in a Culture of Deception

Andy Stanley

In six insight-packed sessions, Andy Stanley exposes four destructive and all-too-prevalent lies about authority, pain, sex, and sin. They're deceptions powerful enough to ruin our relationships, our lives, even our eternities—but only if we let them. Including both a small group DVD and participant's guide that work together, *Twisting the Truth* untwists the lies that can drag us down. With his gift for straight, to-the-heart communication, Andy Stanley helps us exchange falsehoods for truths that can turn our lives completely around.

Available in stores and online!

Starting Point Starter Kit

Find Your Place in the Story

Andy Stanley and the Starting Point Team

Starting Point is an exploration of God's grand story and where you fit into the narrative. This proven, small group experience is carefully designed to meet the needs of

- Seekers that are curious about Christianity
- Starters that are new to a relationship with Jesus
- Returners that have been away from church for a while

Starting Point is an accepting, conversational environment where people learn about God's story and their places in it. Starting Point helps participants explore the Bible and begin to understand key truths of the Christian faith.

Carefully refined to enhance community, the ten interactive sessions in Starting Point encourage honest exploration. The *Conversation Guide*, which includes a five-disk audio series featuring Andy Stanley, helps each participant enjoy and engage fully with the small group experience.

About This Starter Kit

The *Starting Point Starter Kit* is geared for ministry leaders. It consists of the following:

- Four-color *Starting Point Conversation Guide* containing five audio disks, with over five hours of teaching by Andy Stanley
- *Starter Guide* providing step-by-step instructions on how to successfully launch and sustain the Starting Point ministry
- A Starting Point TNIV Bible
- One-hour leader training DVD
- Interactive CD containing promotional videos, pre-service marketing graphics, leader training tools, and administrative resources

Share Your Thoughts

With the Author: Your comments will be forwarded to the author when you send them to *zauthor@zondervan.com*.

With Zondervan: Submit your review of this book by writing to *zreview@zondervan.com*.

Free Online Resources at
www.zondervan.com

Zondervan AuthorTracker: Be notified whenever your favorite authors publish new books, go on tour, or post an update about what's happening in their lives at www.zondervan.com/authortracker.

Daily Bible Verses and Devotions: Enrich your life with daily Bible verses or devotions that help you start every morning focused on God. Visit www.zondervan.com/newsletters.

Free Email Publications: Sign up for newsletters on Christian living, academic resources, church ministry, fiction, children's resources, and more. Visit www.zondervan.com/newsletters.

Zondervan Bible Search: Find and compare Bible passages in a variety of translations at www.zondervanbiblesearch.com.

Other Benefits: Register yourself to receive online benefits like coupons and special offers, or to participate in research.

ZONDERVAN®

ZONDERVAN.com/
AUTHORTRACKER
follow your favorite authors